Las Aventuras de Marvino

Works by Marvin Hill

A Mediocre Life

Las Aventuras de Marvino

Las Aventuras de Marvino

Illustrated and Written by:

Marvin Hill

Las Aventuras de Marvino

ISBN-13: 978-1507704882

ISBN-10: 1507704887

For more information:

Visit the author's blog: www.marvhill.com

Dedicated to my Mother,

Virginia Rodriguez Hill,

Who has always put up with my shit.

You have been, and always will be,

My Rock.

Also, I'm pretty sure you bought me my first crayons.

LAS AVENTURAS de MARVINO

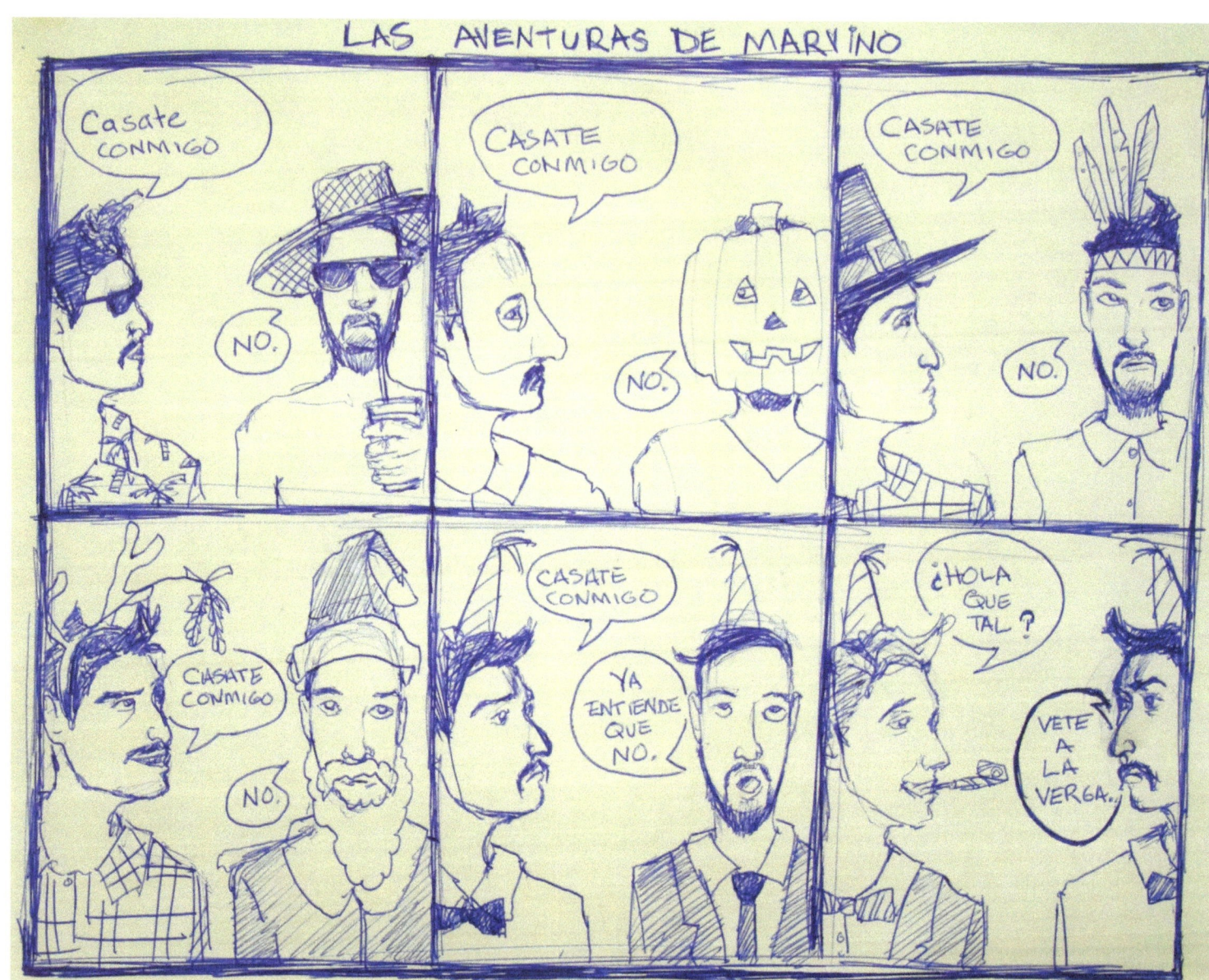

LAS AVENTURAS de MARVIÑO

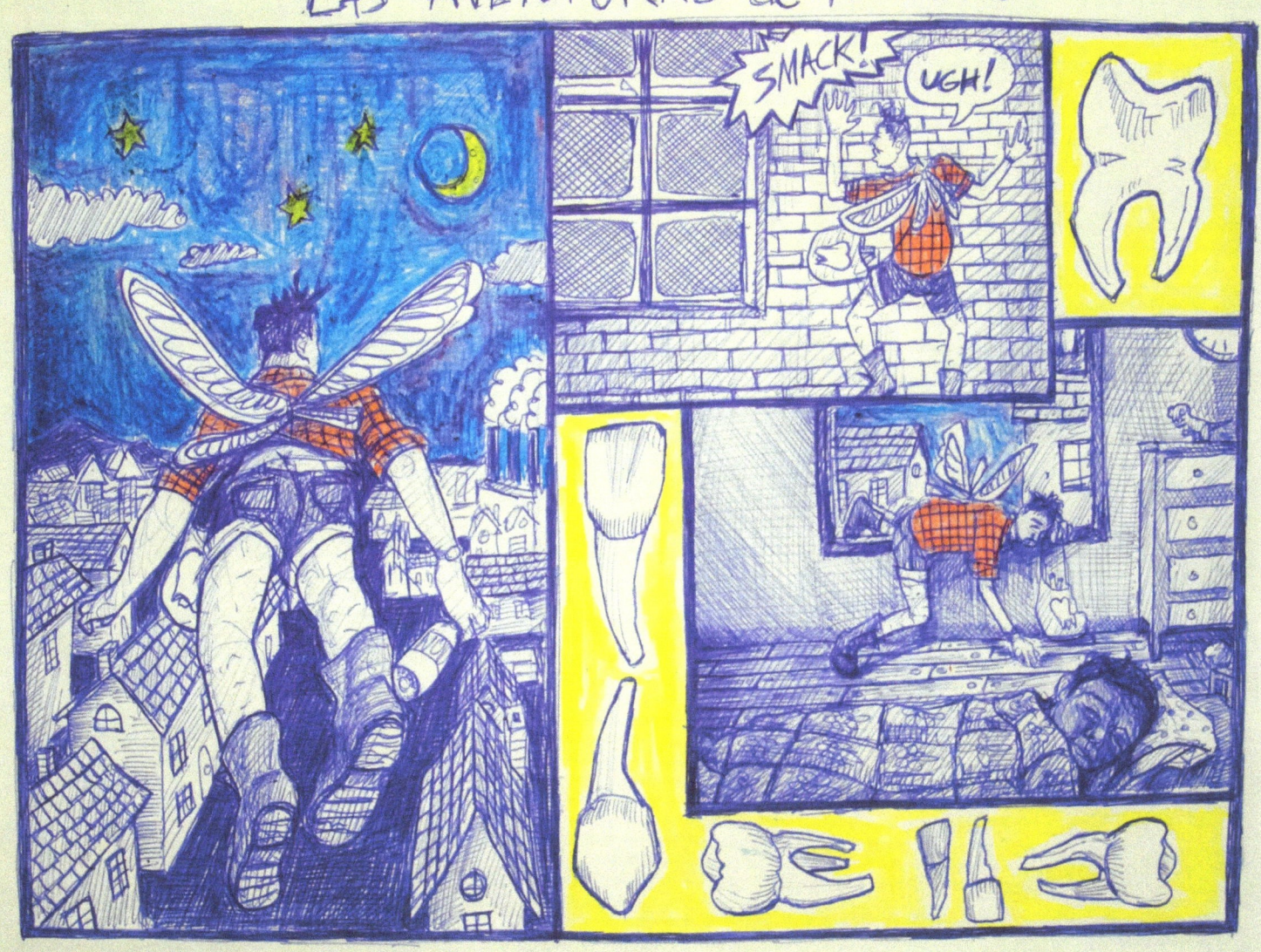

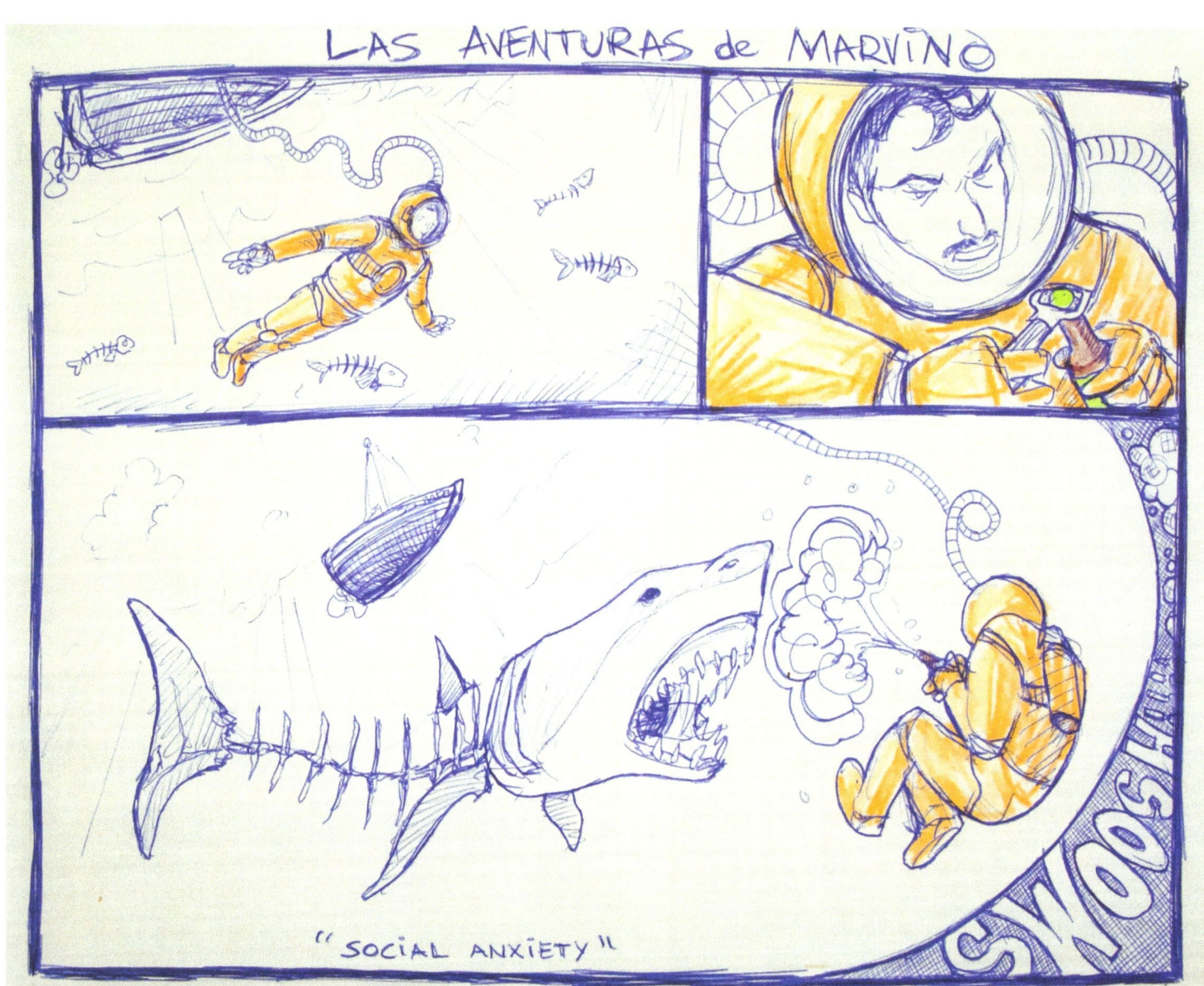

"SOCIAL ANXIETY"

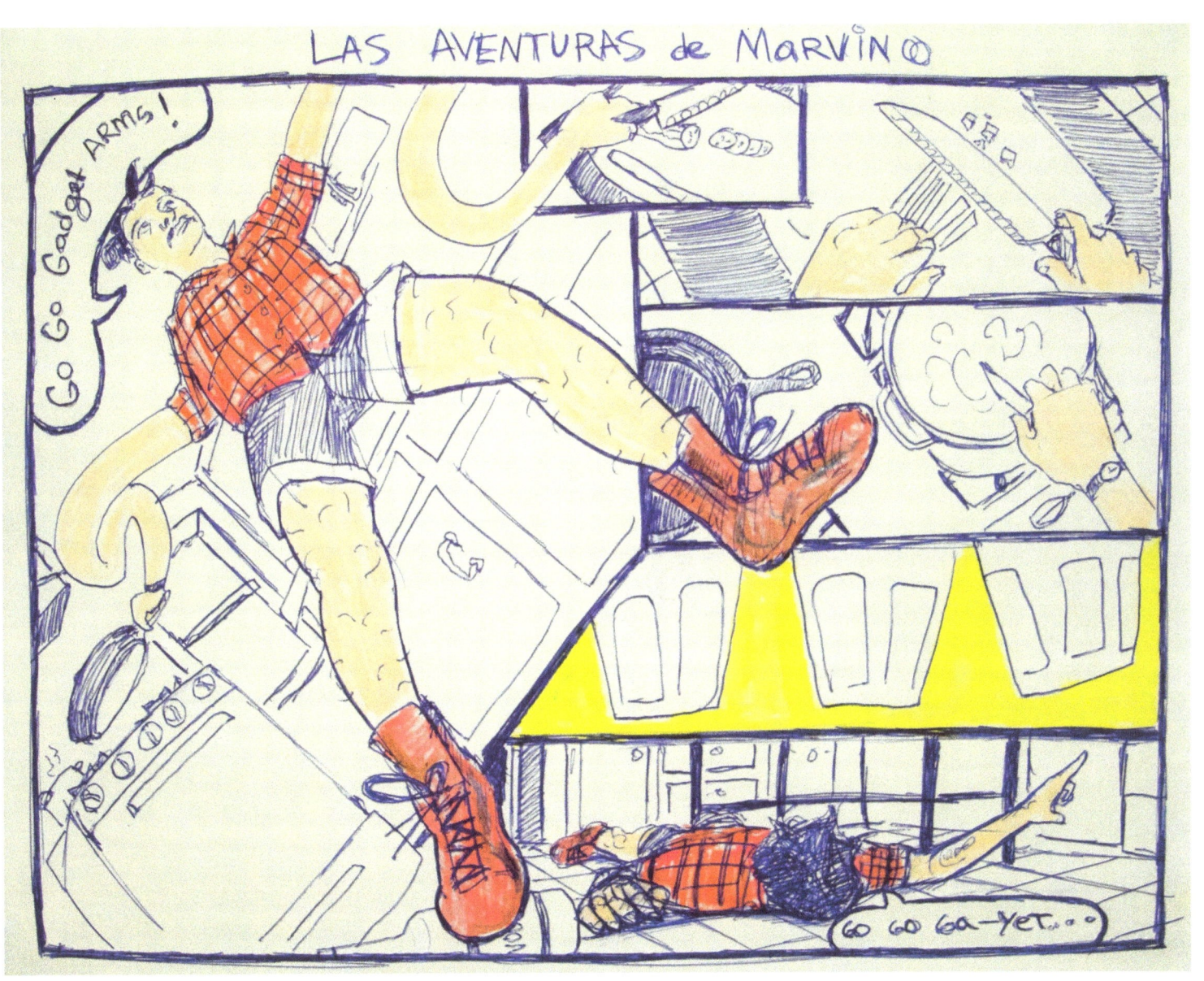

11

LAS AVENTURAS de MARVIÑO

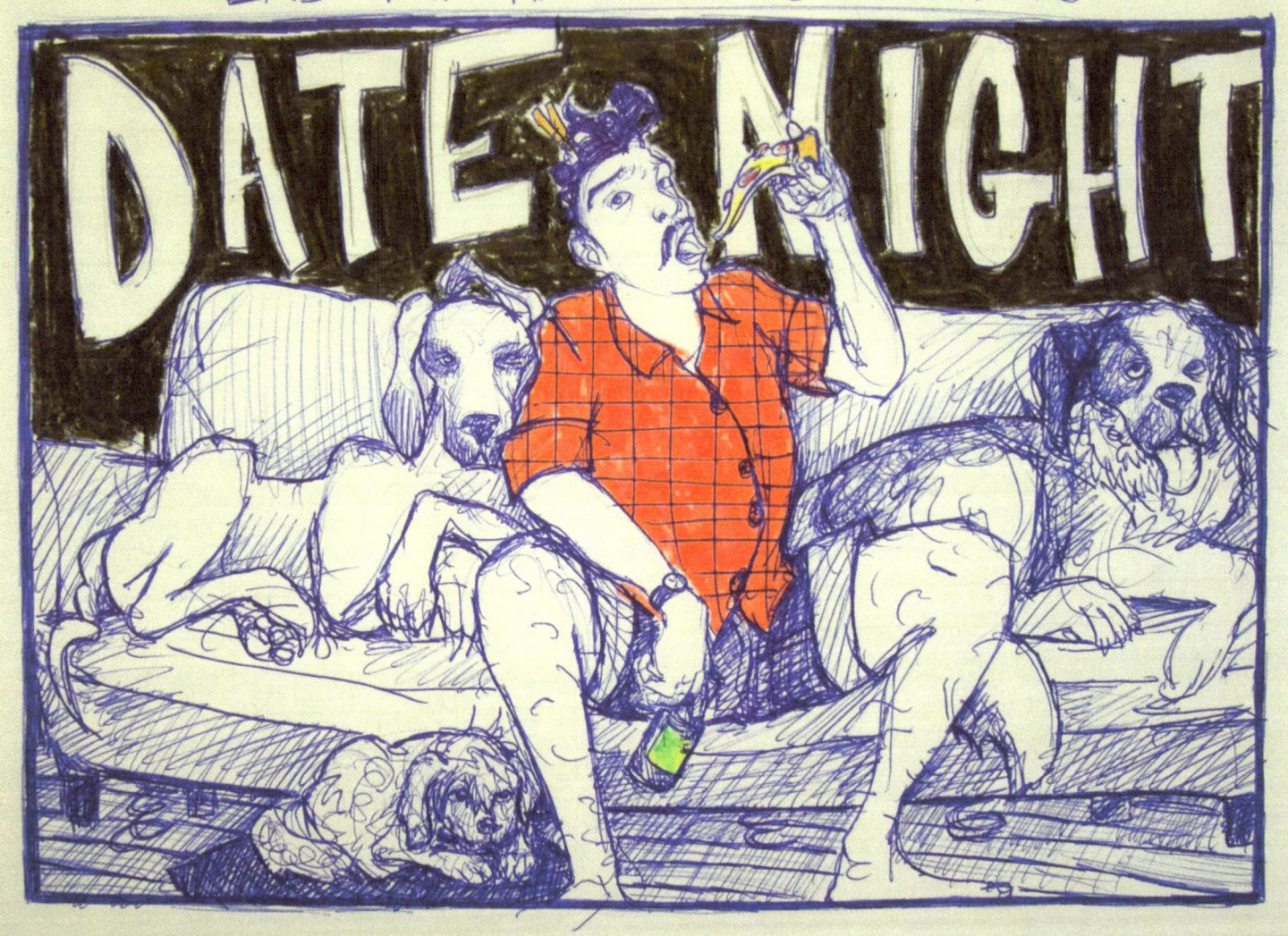

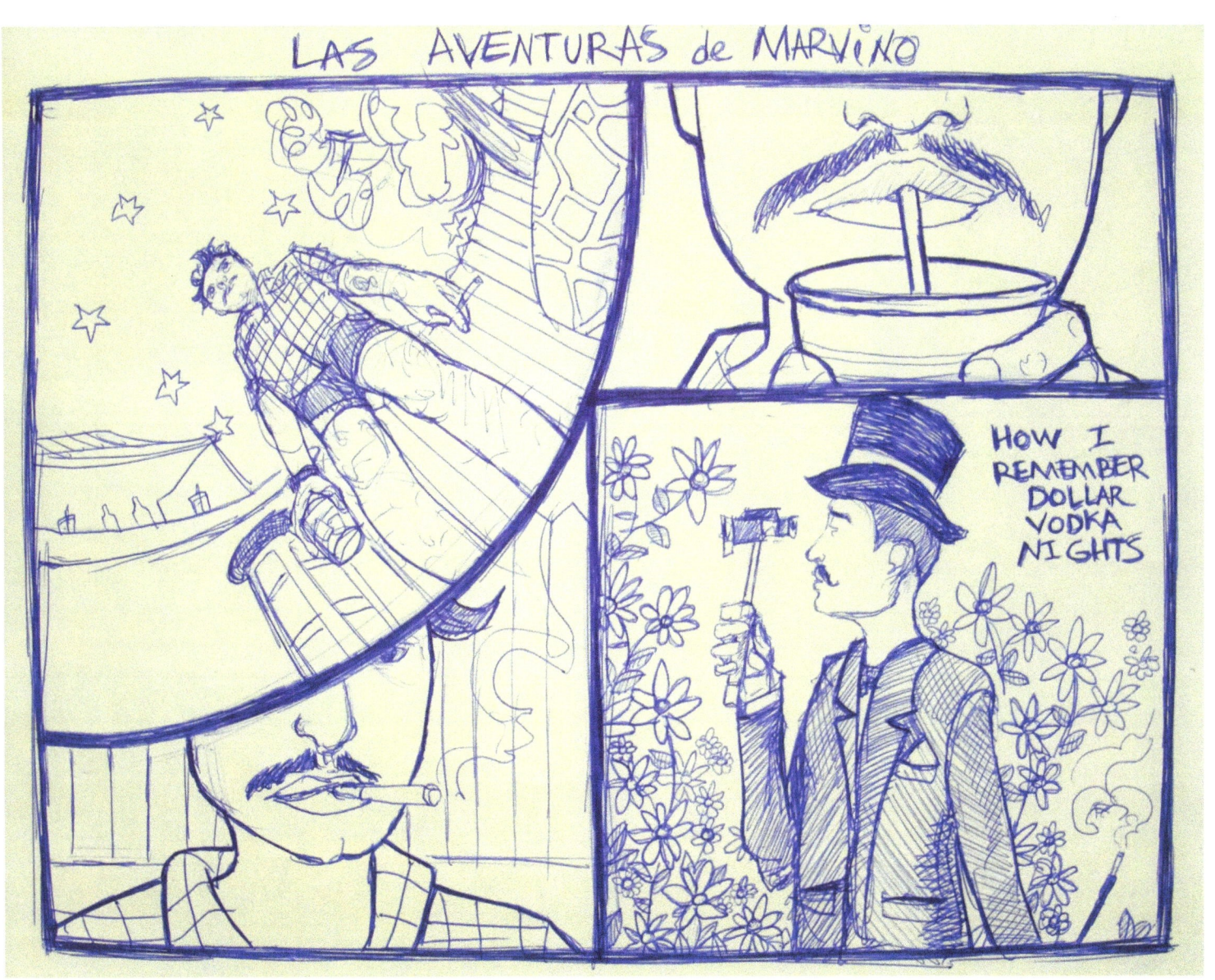

LAS AVENTURAS de MARVINO

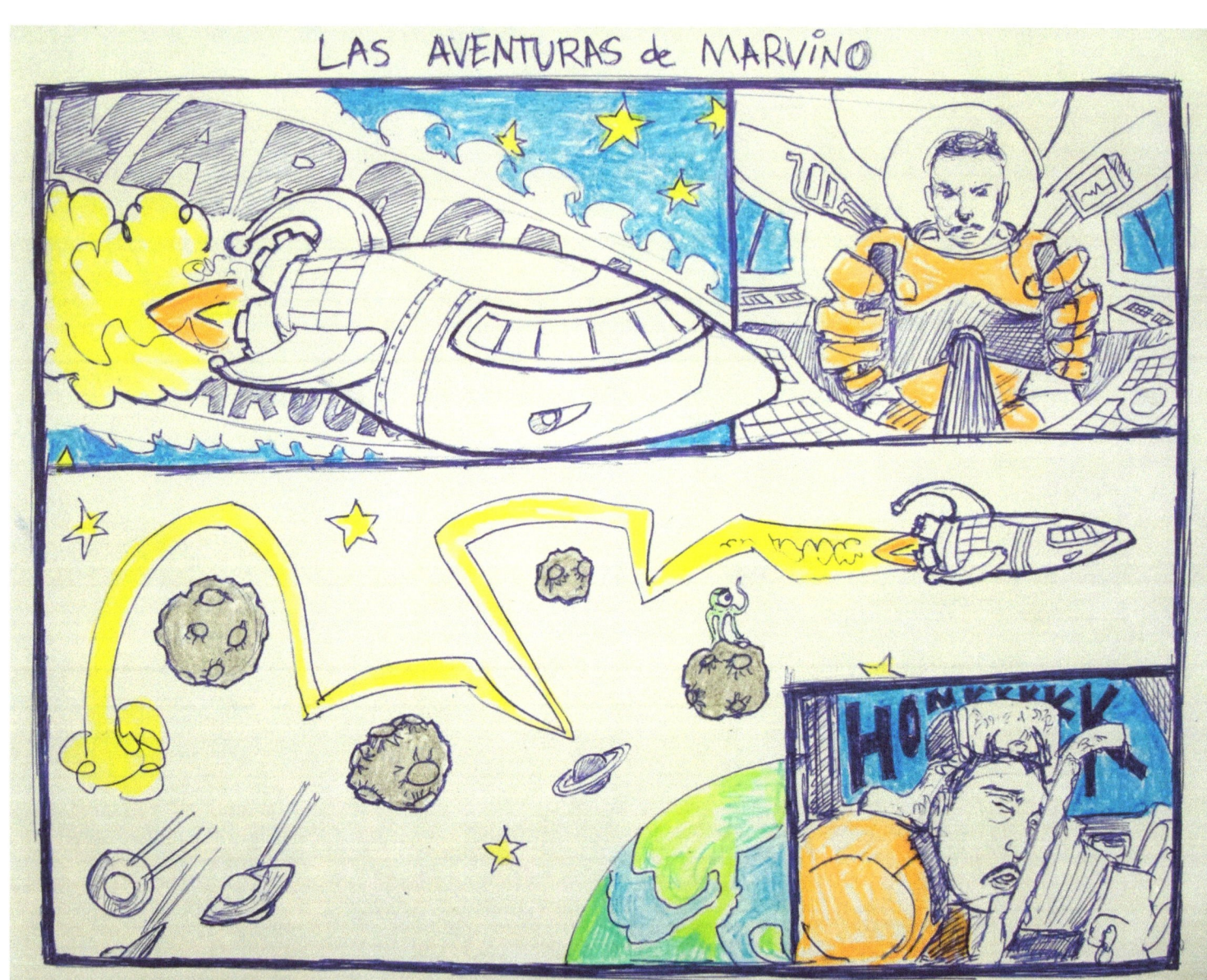

14

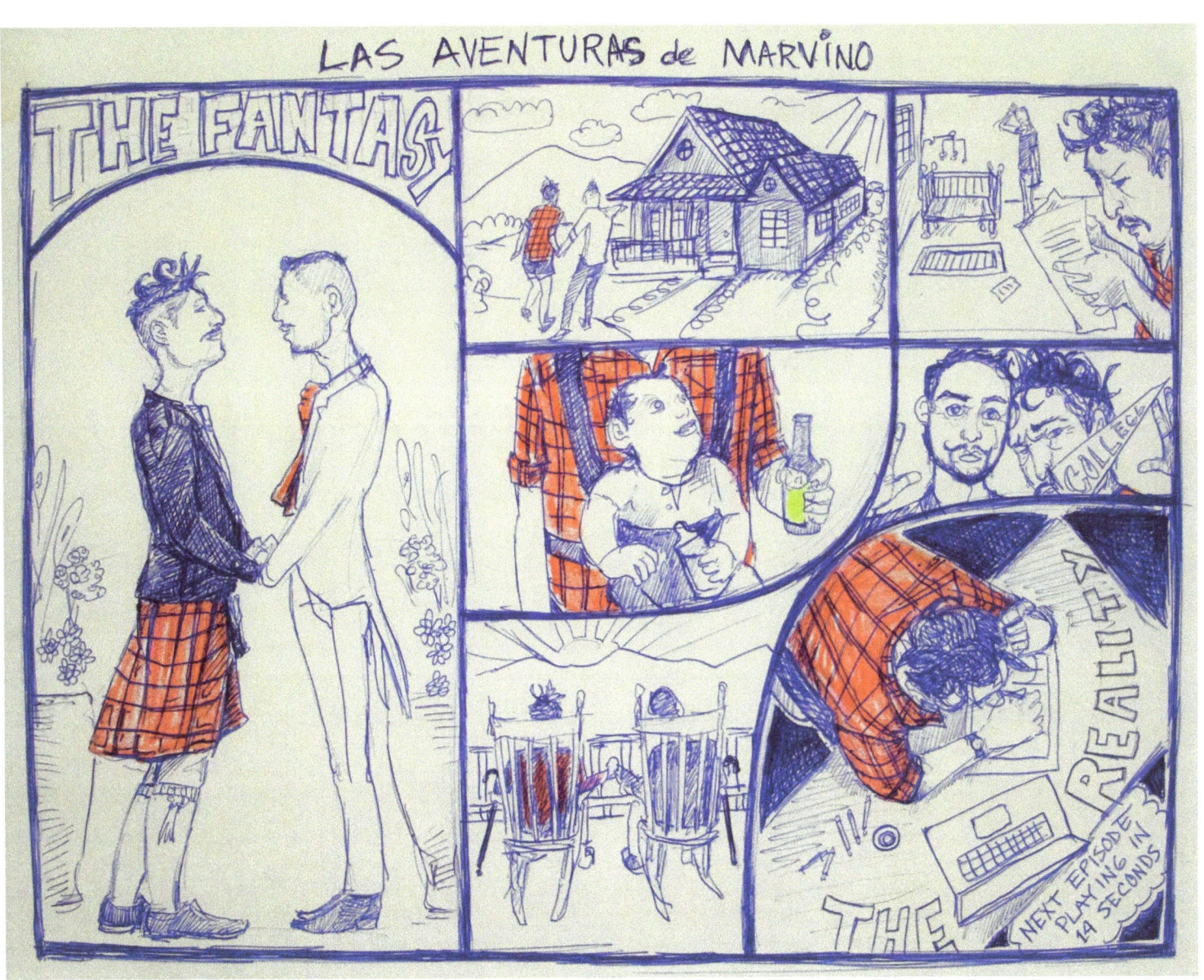

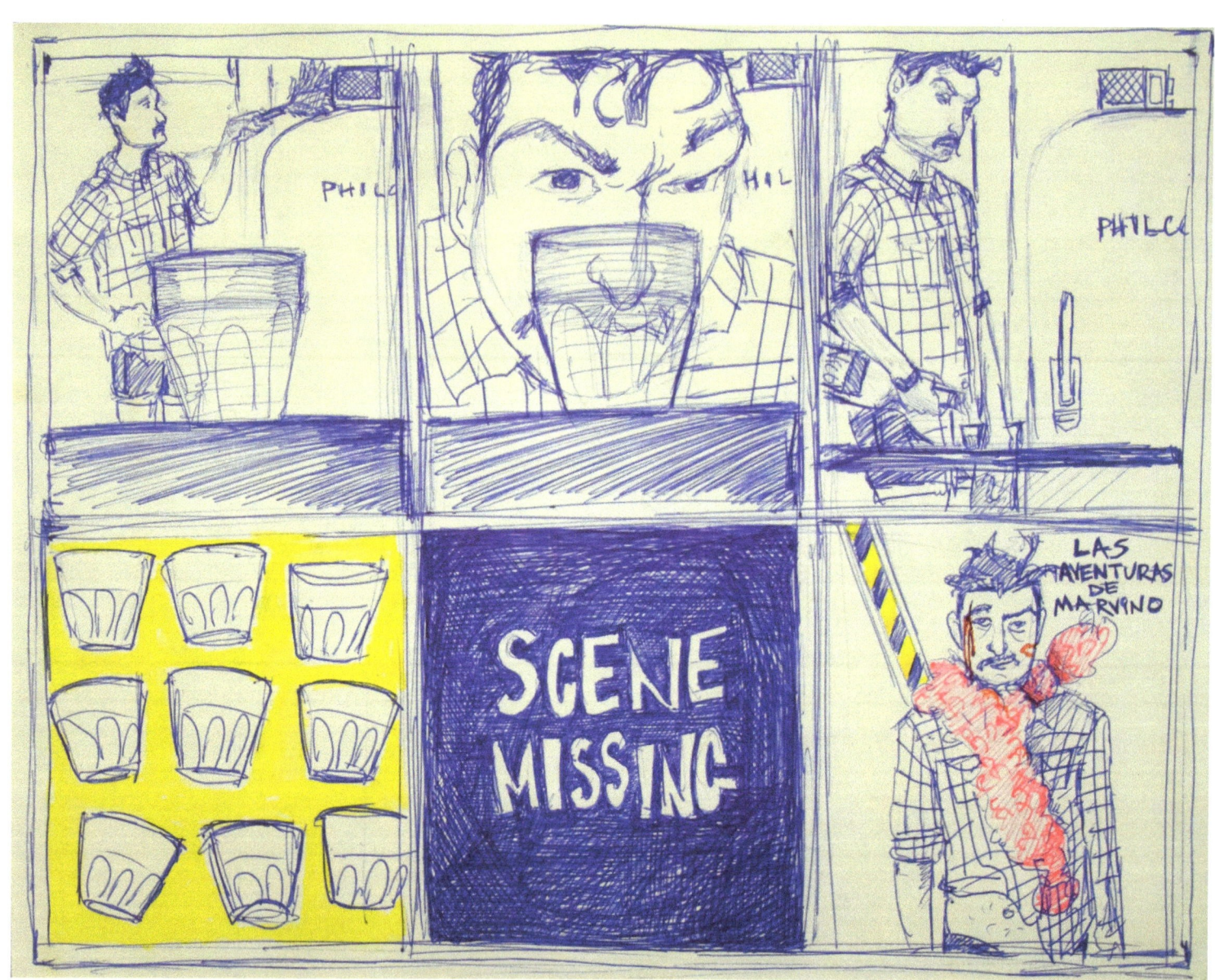

16

LAS AVENTURAS de MARVINO

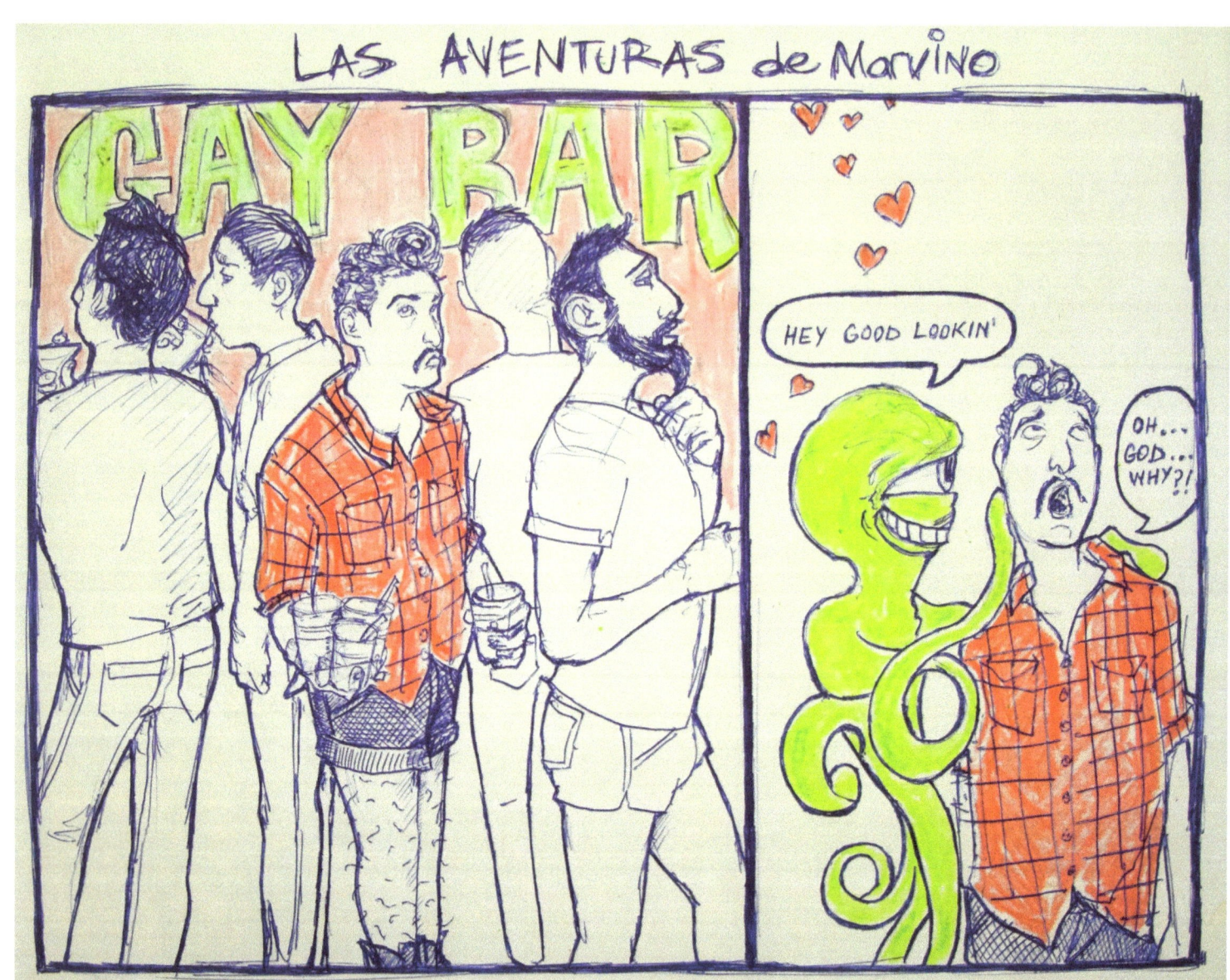

LAS AVENTURAS de MARVINO

LAS AVENTURAS de MARVINO

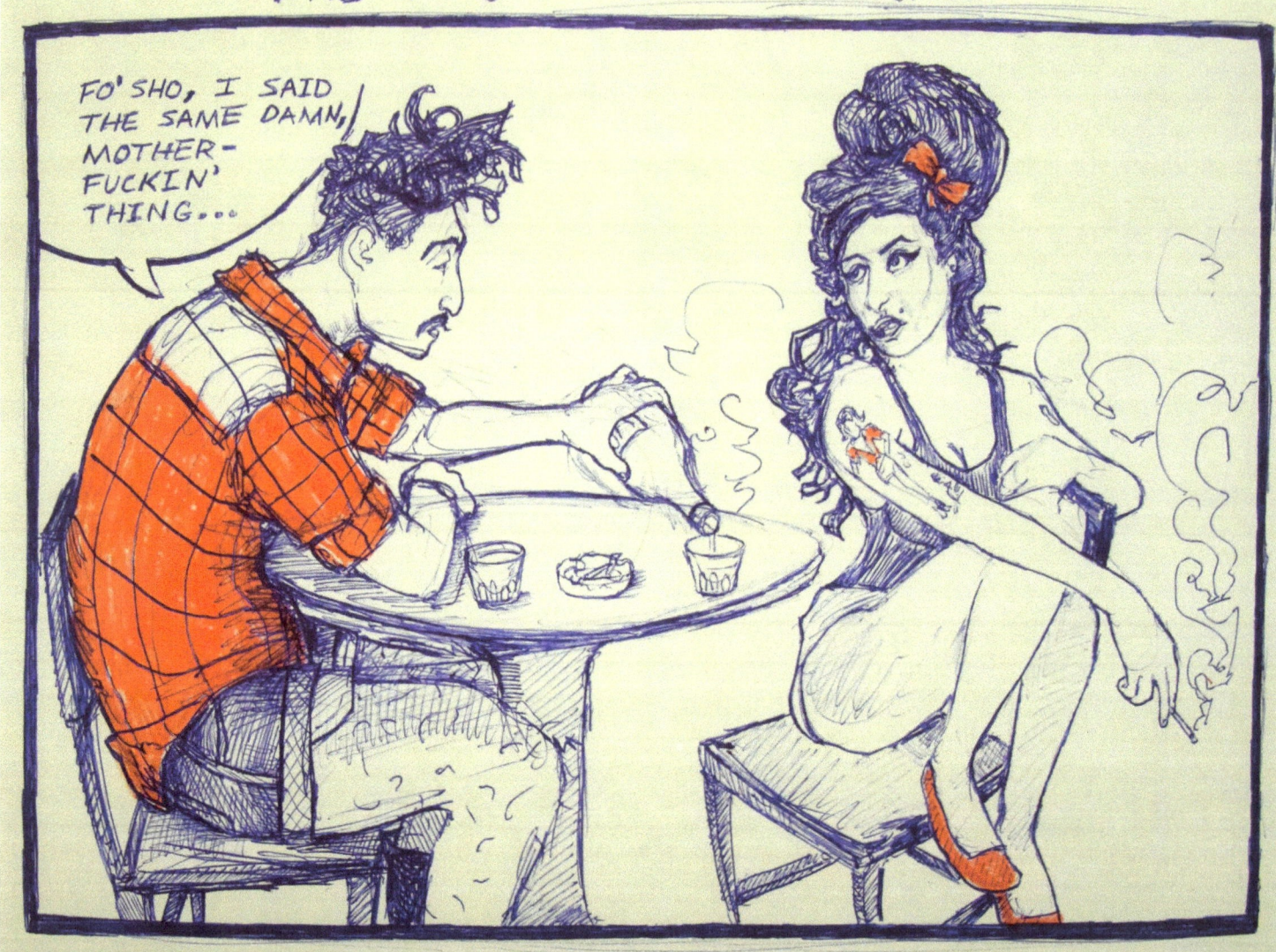

LAS AVENTURAS de MARVINO

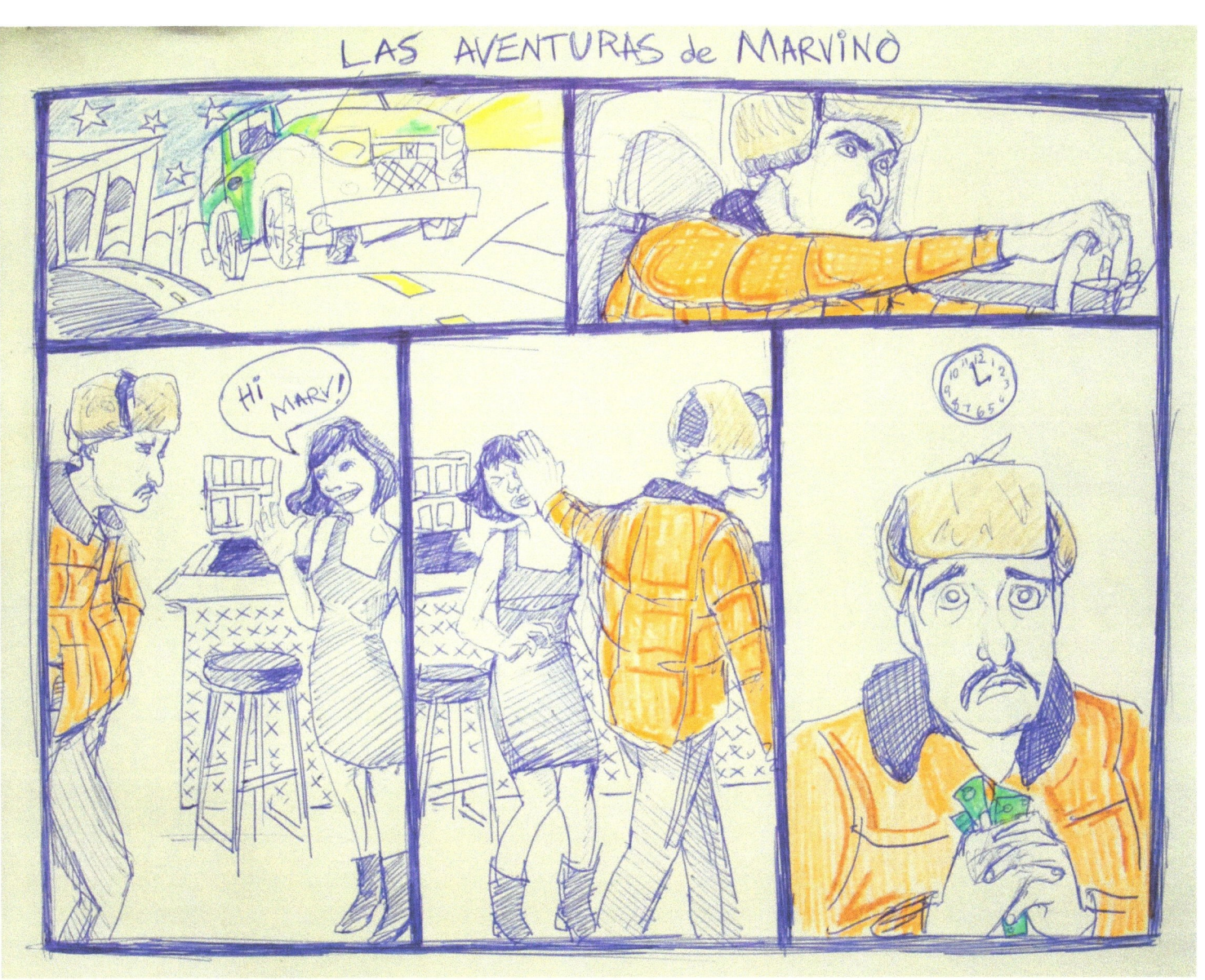

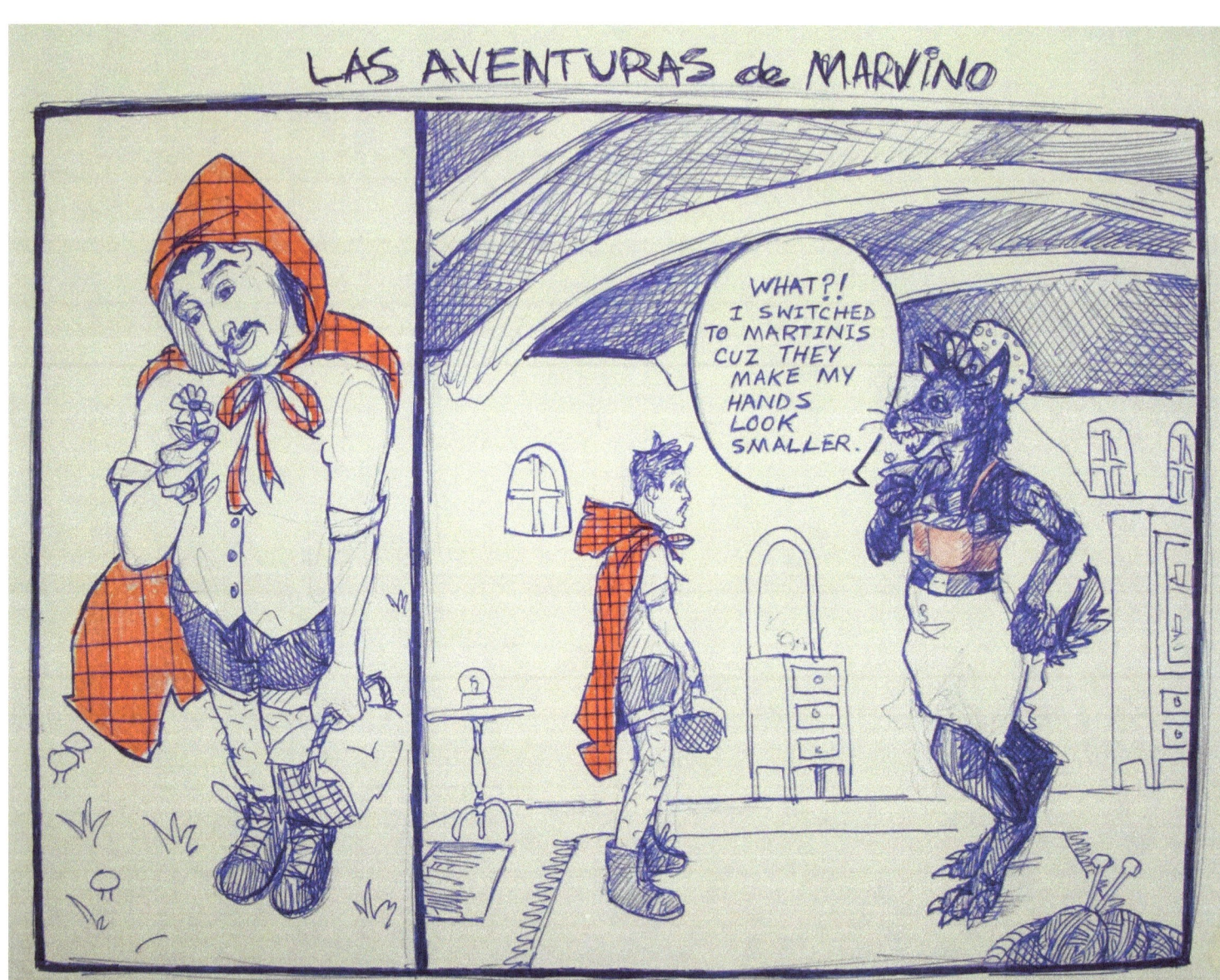

LAS AVENTURAS de Marviño

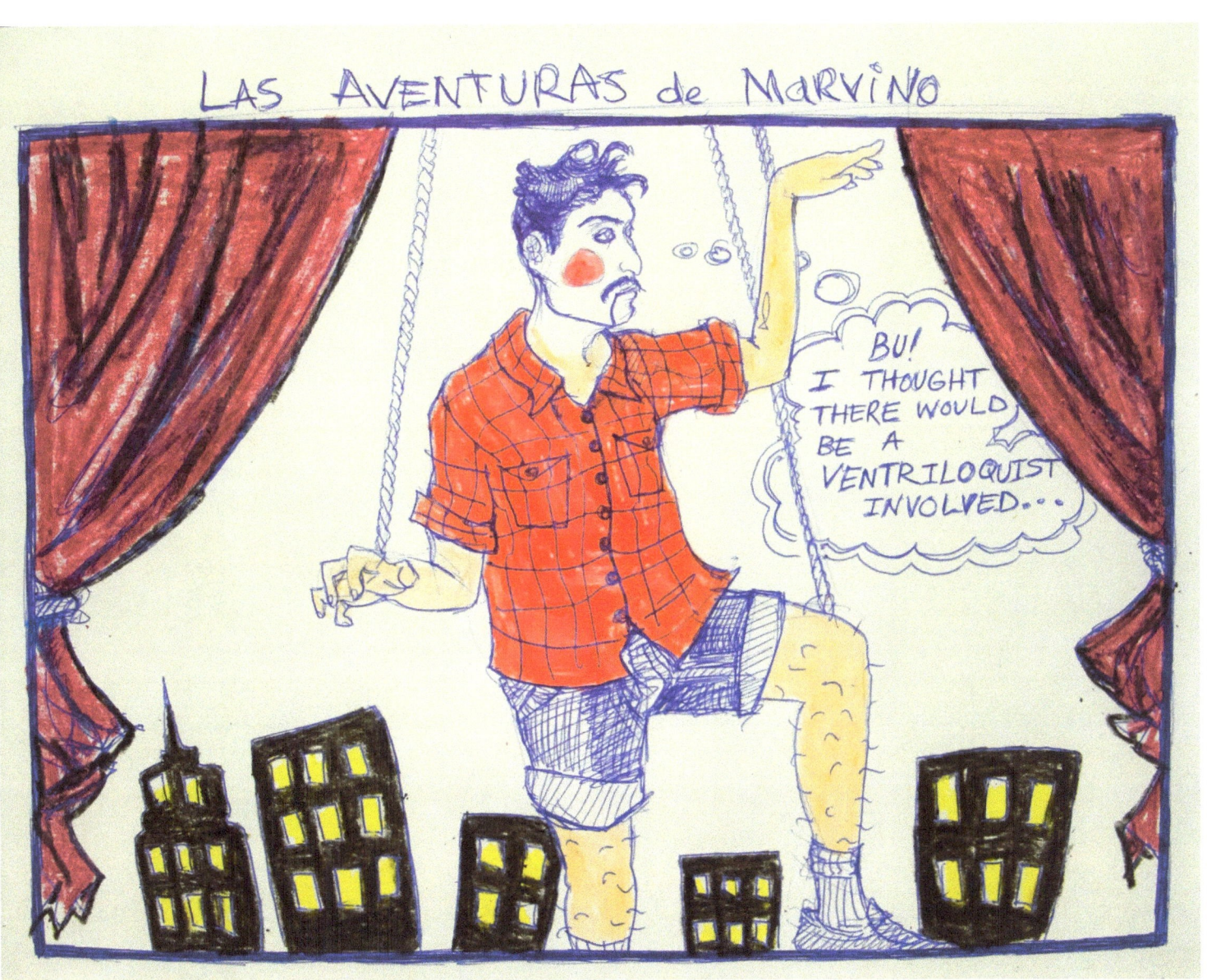

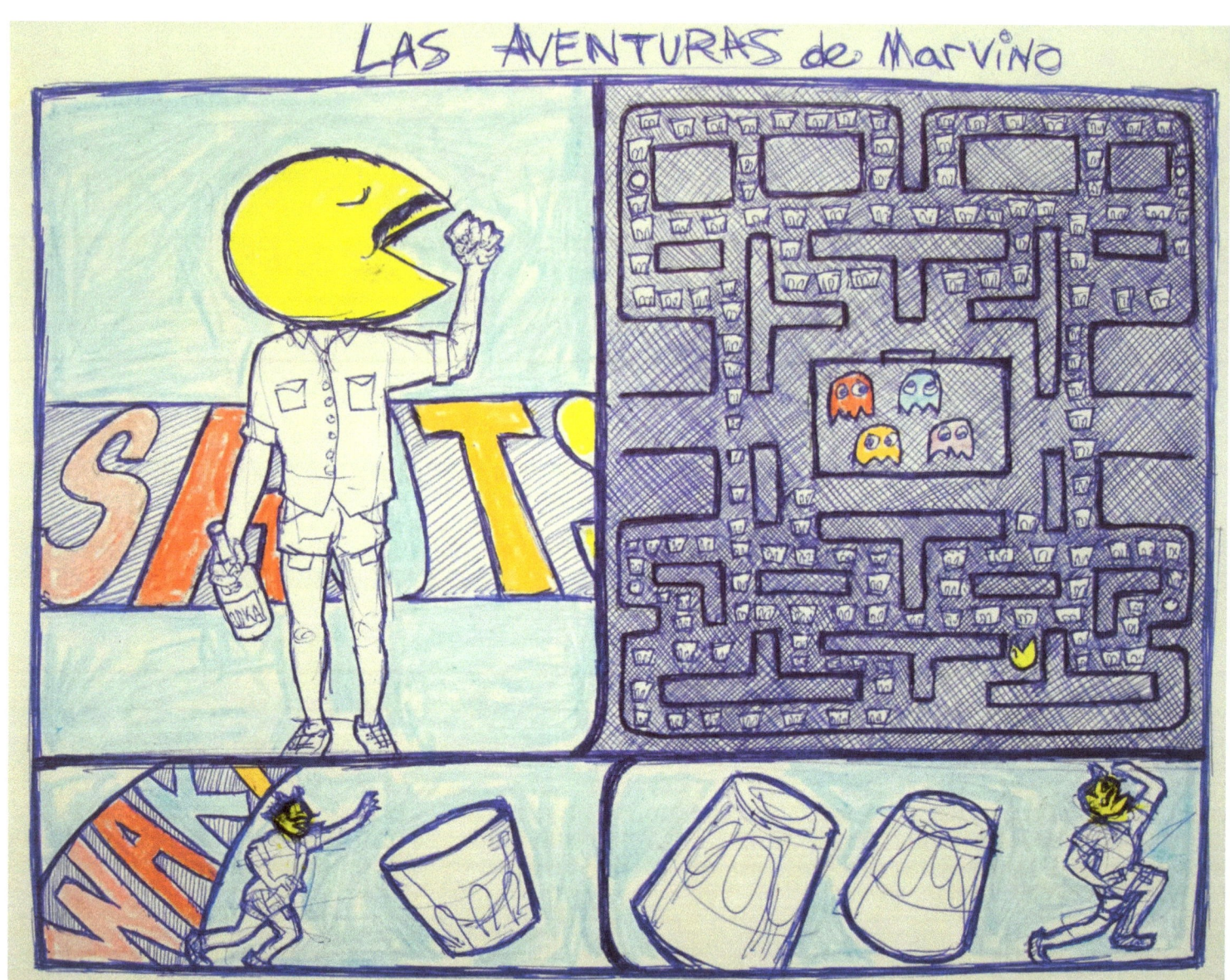

24

LAS AVENTURAS de MARVINO

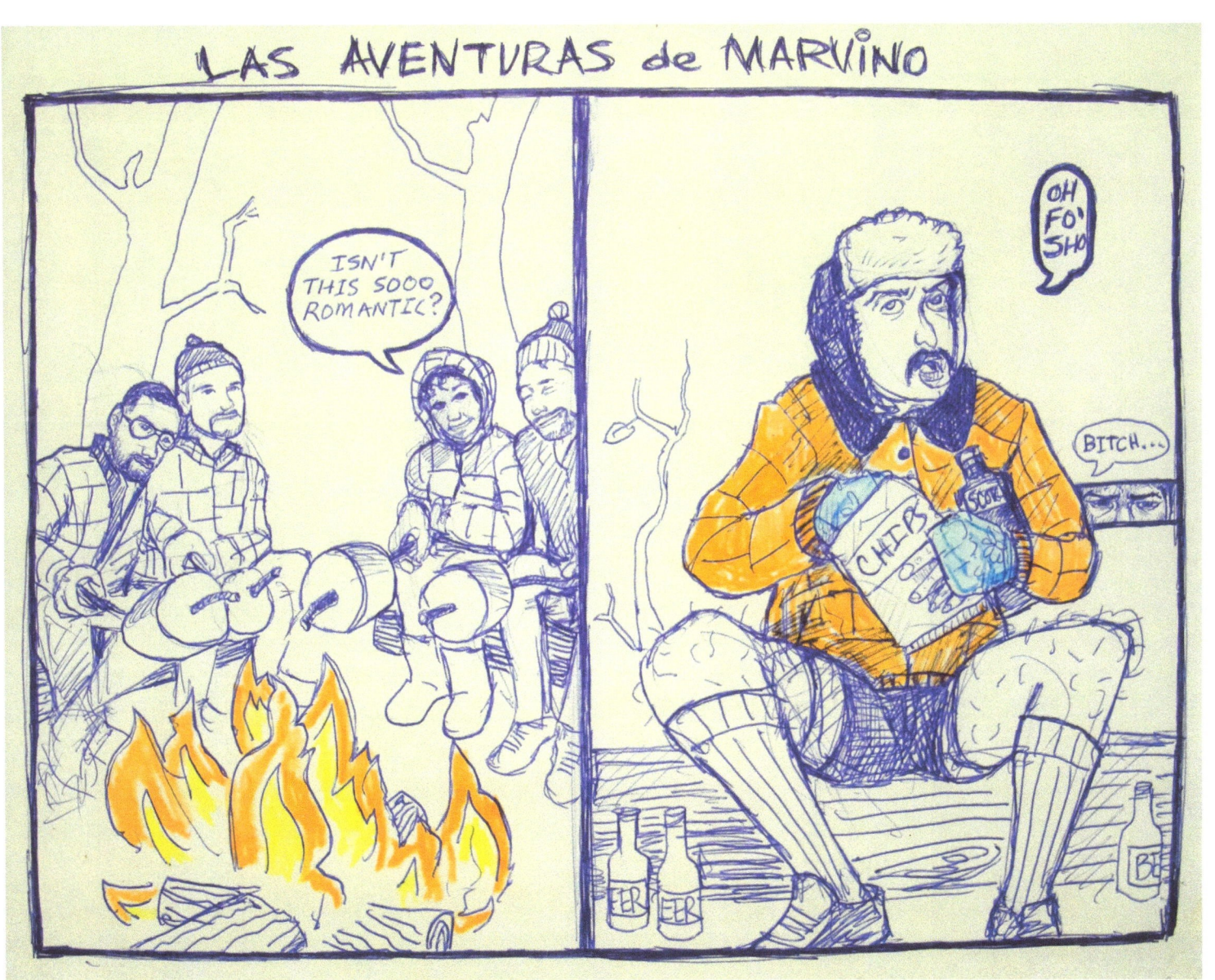

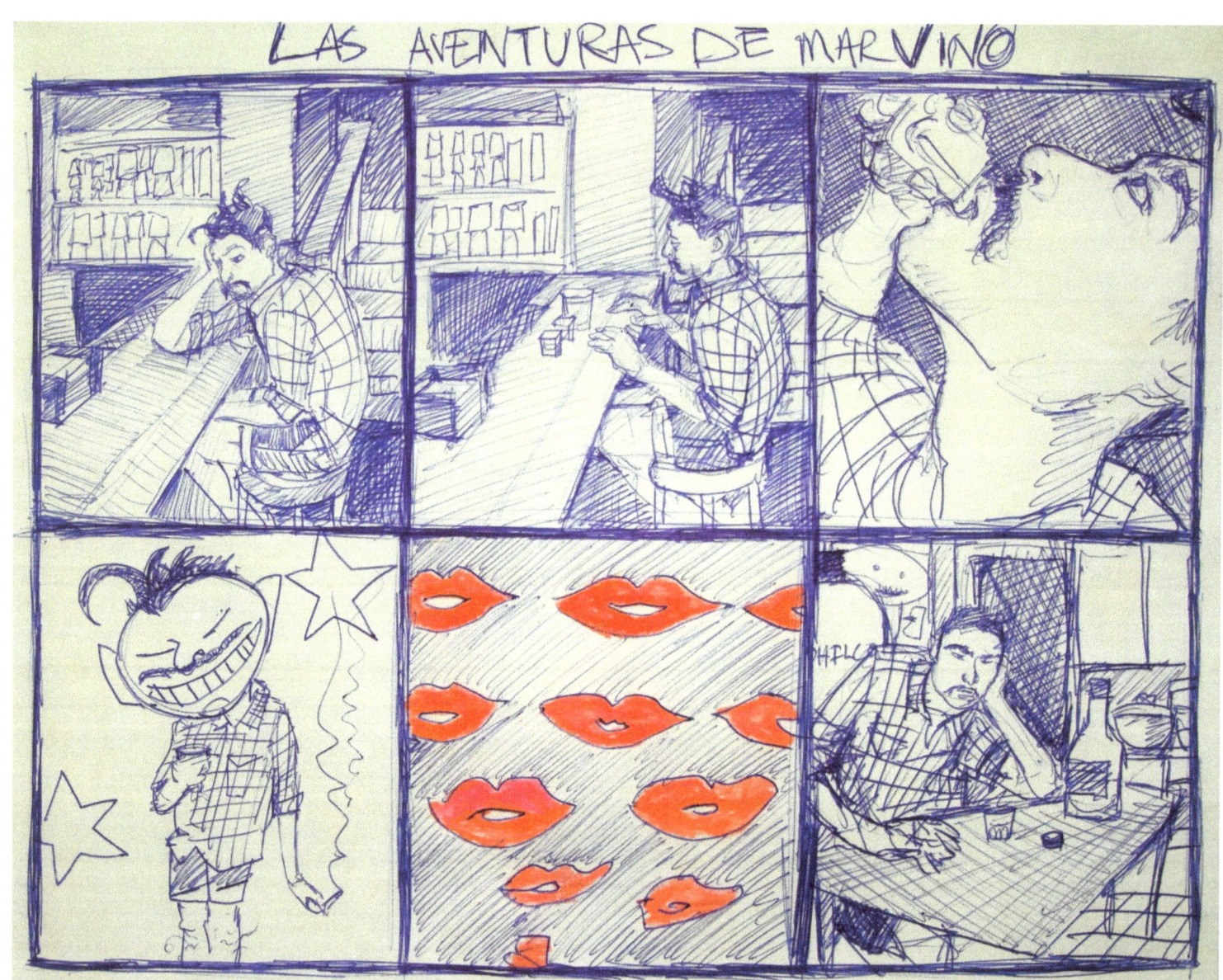

LAS AVENTURAS de MARVINO

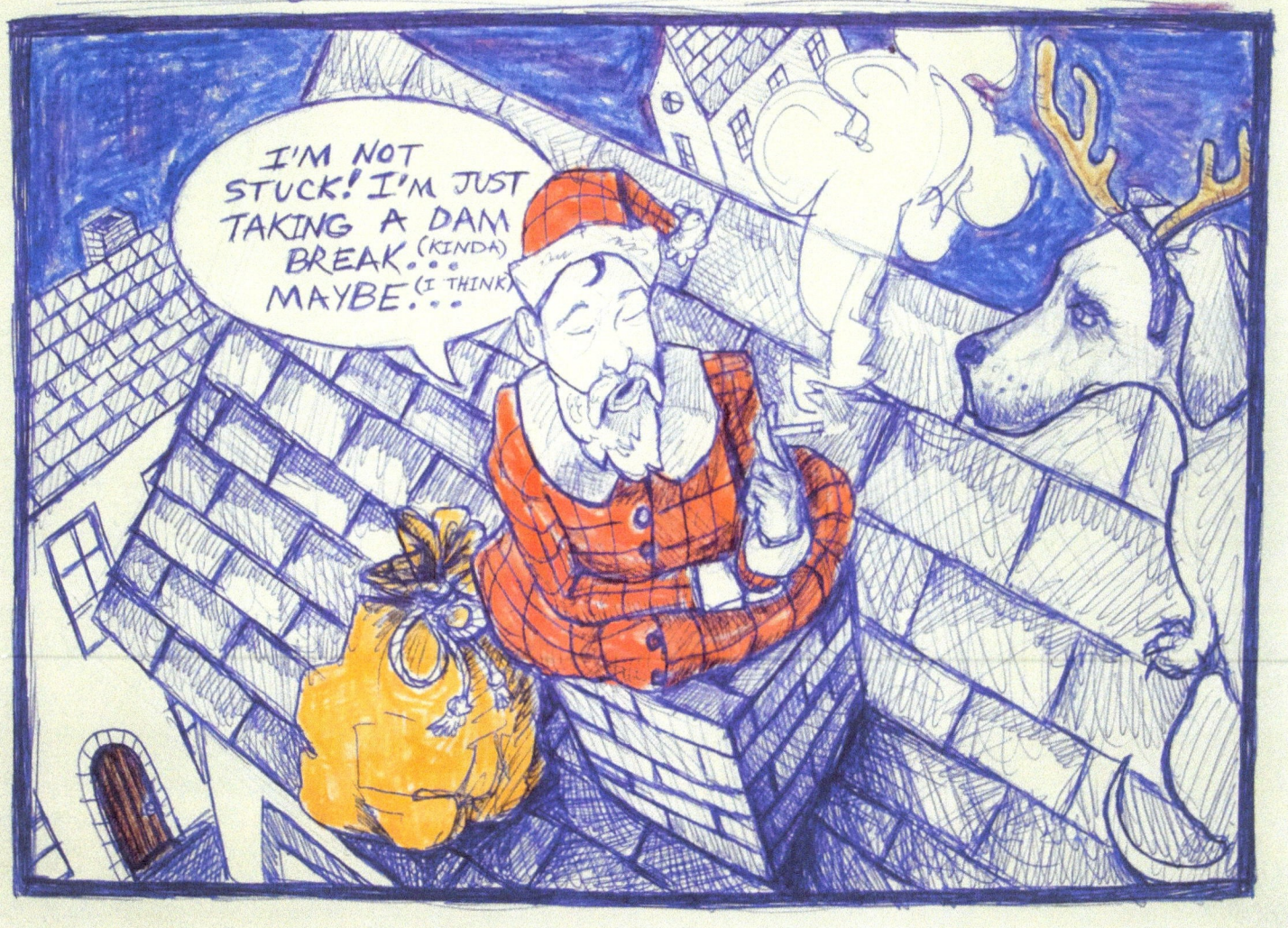

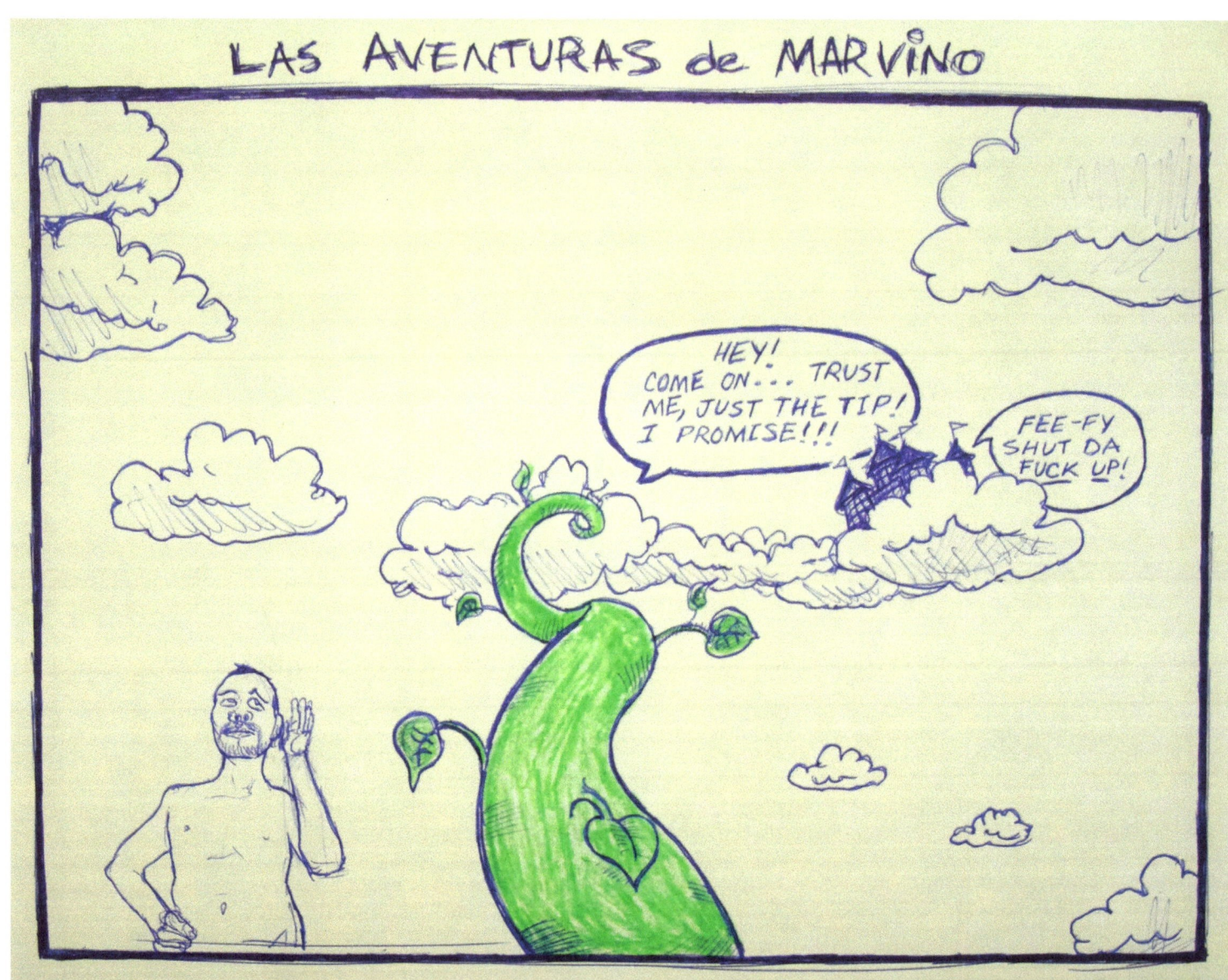

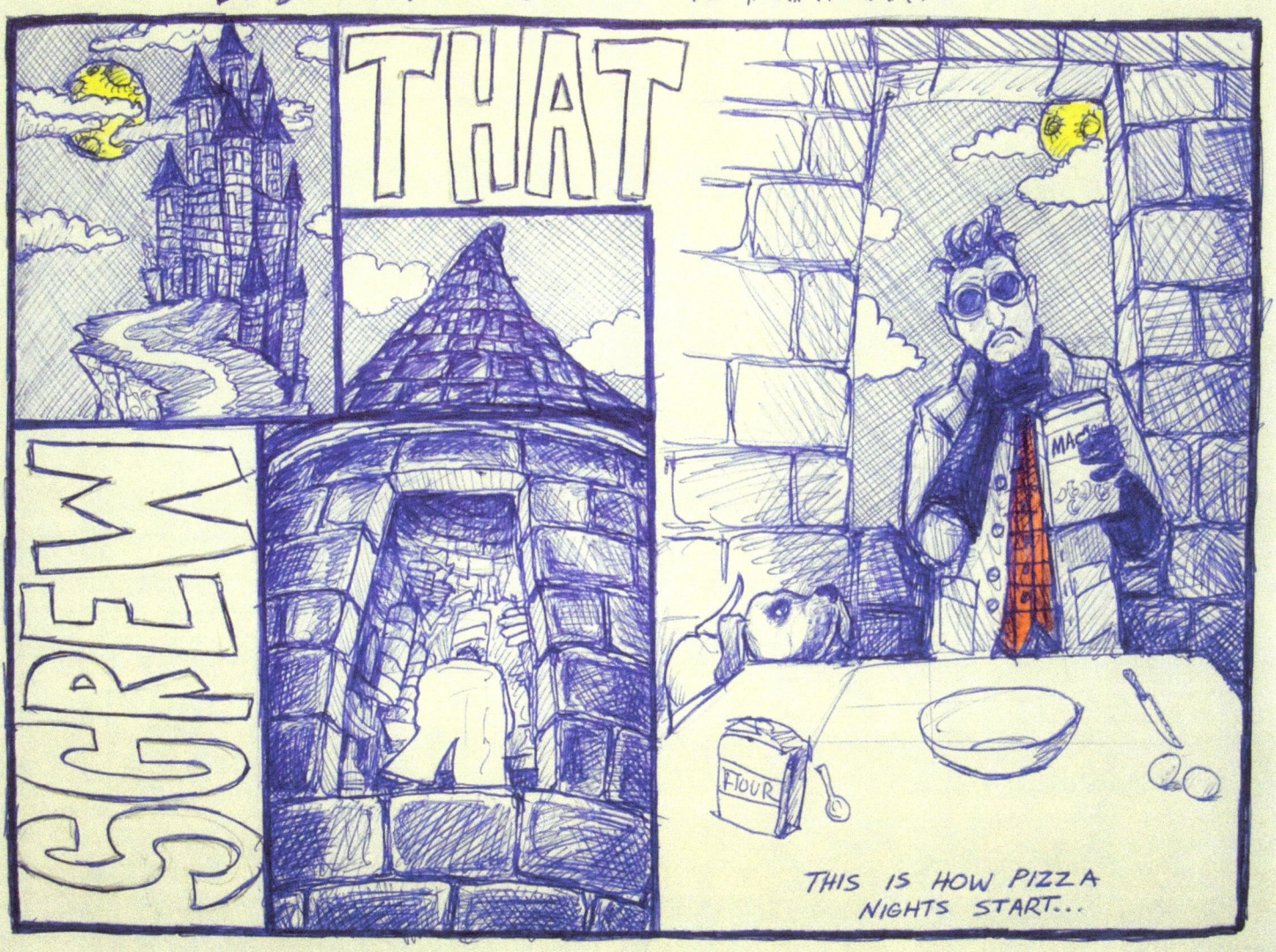

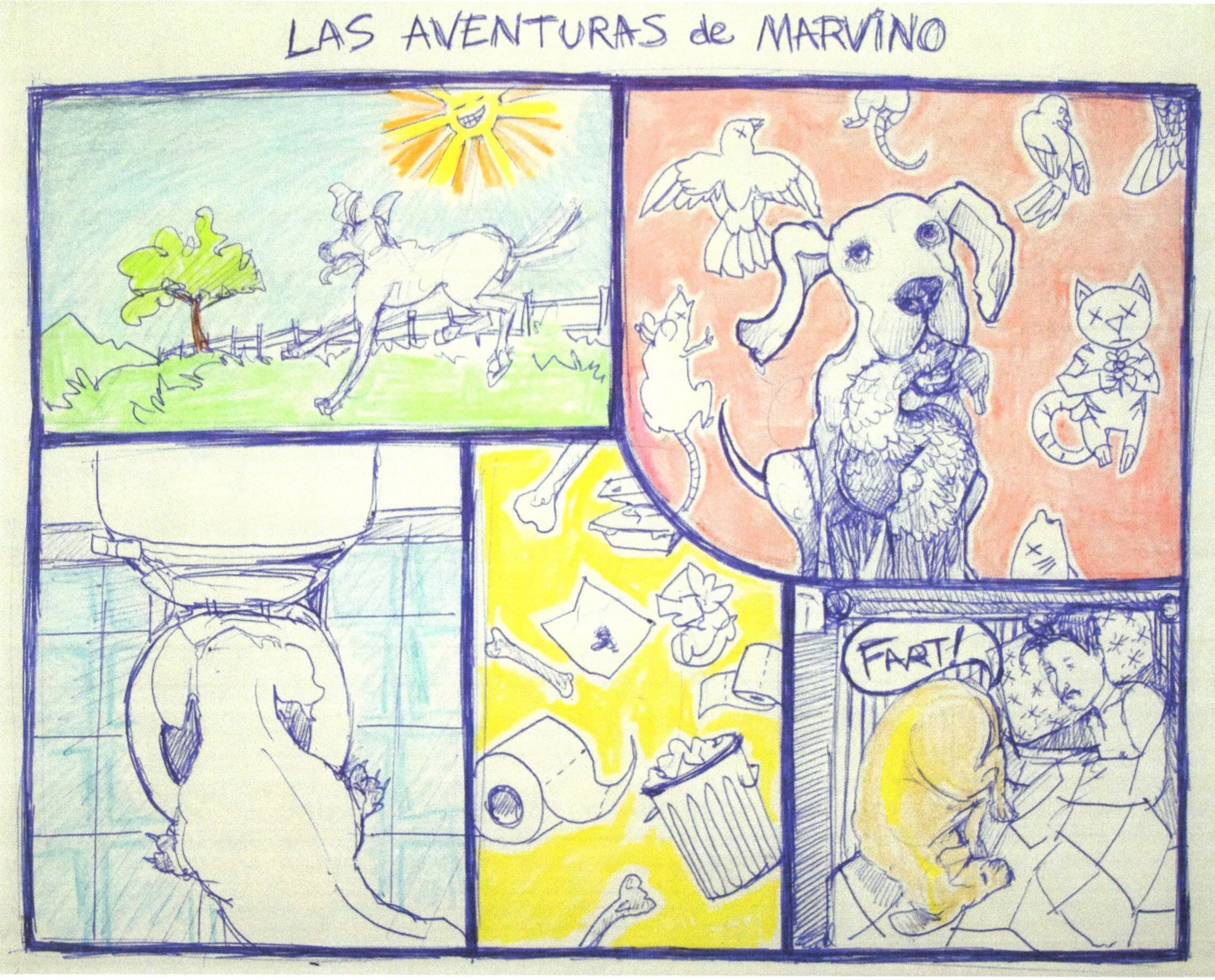

LAS AVENTURAS de MARVINO

To all the adventures that lay ahead

www.ingramcontent.com/pod-product-compliance
Lightning Source LLC
Chambersburg PA
CBHW050909180526
45159CB00007B/2851